A LITTL
A WHC

Liz Barnes has written for as long as she can remember. She has now produced hundreds of poems, children's stories, adult short stories, and a novel.

It was since taking Parkinson's medication that her writing has become prolific and, she, slightly obsessive. When Liz is not writing she is being a social worker, painting or making things from wire. Her twenty odd years of social work clearly influence her poetry. She also enjoys participating in some of the local open mic nights around Brighton and West Sussex.

Her work is unique and highly emotive.

Liz says:
'My writing may be drug induced but it's my saviour, my friend, my therapy, my time waster and what keeps me out of trouble.'

A little bit of *pain* and a whole lot of *love*

Liz Barnes

THE REAL PRESS
www.therealpress.co.uk

Published in 2022 by the Real Press.
www.therealpress.co.uk
© Liz Barnes

ISBN (print) 9781912119400
ISBN (ebooks) 9781912119394

Cover artwork by Liz Barnes.

For anyone that lessens the pain and adds to the love.

Contents

Chapter 1

Changes

I didn't know what love was before I met my current partner. I thought I did, but I was wrong. Now I do and it's very different to what I experienced before.

Getting hurt and separating from my fiancé was the best thing that could have happened. New relationships are a bit scary, and change is anxiety provoking but, nearly every time I have had a change in my life, it has been for the better.

When this all happened, I was working with young offenders, a challenging but great bunch of kids who I really enjoyed getting to know. I found them full of character and life and that once you understood them you could see why they had taken a wrong turn. This job made me feel like a grown up for the first time which is why I've included 'Top of the Pops and Flip Flops'. Being and feeling like an adult makes you reflect on your childhood.

My nan was a constant in my life and very precious to me. I wish she could see this book; she would have been brimming with pride. She only met my new partner a few times but when she took her hand and held onto it, I knew she approved.

Memories in Flight

The little magpie that sits upon the dry grass
Resembles my nan with its black headscarf
Pecking away just like she would nibble at a cheese sarnie
Walking head down, watching its feet
It amuses me as it turns around
Pecks some more at nothing on the ground
Its wings at first held firmly by its side
Then it flutters and dances before taking flight
And I am reminded of how my nan danced
Her feet moved with such elegance
I used to watch her entranced
How she glided and swished across the ballroom floor
She only felt old when she couldn't dance any more
I watch the little bird as it rests silently on the post
I swear it looks me in the eye, really looks at me and sees
My gratitude, as I thank it for the happy memories

Top of the Pops and Flip Flops

Gascoigne crying,
Ben Johnson lying,
Magic Johnson flying.
Pixie boots,
Bat wing jumpers and a corkscrew perm,
Detention, essay end of term.
Hi Tech, low tech, top by Lonsdale,
Hi top trainers, Hi viz socks,
Crop tops.
Adidas and Nike,
BMX for your bikey.
Woolworths' tunics, pic n mix,
Right Price, The Price is Right,
Top of the Pops, flip flops.
Black eye, left hook,
School fight, homework book.
Kids from Fame,
Operation Game,
Smoking on the school bus.
Playing Twister, hating my sister,
Bull's Eye and Dusty Bin.
Ghostbusters, ET,
Monster Munch for 10p.
Hooch and 2 Dogs, never gin,
Rubix Cube, boob tube, The Tube, being rude.
The Caramac Bunny,

French and Saunders were funny.
Tie and blazer,
Casio watch,
Spots.
Lads being wallies, racing in trollies, rocket lollies.
Walkman, Pacman, Packamac and He-Man,
Mum's gone to Bejam.

Belonging

She was chucked out young, violent dad got real mad.
Useless mum tried to be fun but was drunk and coz she was,
           she weren't no good.
So, she found her blood on the street, sweet.
She fit in more than she had before,
Somewhere to go when low.
Felt safe, nice,
Until she paid the price.
Just one hit, see matchstick lit,
She's scared but bare fear ain't no good.
The first time made her choke, but he said inhale as her face
           went pale,
So she took the smoke, felt dope.
The hook that reeled her in would always win, flame on tin
Plenty of sin to buy the stuff.
Enough's enough but she can't stop.
Pop a pill.
No will to carry on but it's done,
No fun.
She always felt sad and now she believes she's bad.
Mad days spent raising dough, staying low,
Feds know her name, her game,
Her only fame the photo they took when they locked her up
           in a cell, living hell and her mates fell aside, said
           she had no pride, told lies, so friendship died and
           now she's alone.

She was wrong, they weren't her bros, just scum that waits
for prey.
That lay their traps hoping your need will benefit their greed.
She's in and out looks old,
Sold her soul years ago to thrills, cold turkey chills.
The short lived high and no one waves goodbye as she takes
her last draw and hits the floor.
Toxic rocks dock and fill her blood with poison.
Her heart stops beating, defeating her body and mind.
I wish her death was rare but it's no news no need for clues.
Police won't bother just ring her mother and when she's
sober, she says she told her.
Then gets drunk and scores some skunk from the very same
bloke that gave her daughter her first high.
She thinks he's just another guy.
And all she wanted was to belong.

Messages from Society

I think we are okay, say the messages from society.
I cook dinner whilst he rejects sobriety.
I earn the money which he drinks with his mates.
Pay the bills and send cheques for council rates.
He's just a cheeky chappie who likes to flirt a bit.
I hoover and polish and cook, housework here is never split.
He's a man, I should be proud, a real man.
He drinks lager with his tea,
In front of the TV, for which I pay the licence fee.
He likes new clothes, which I buy,
Because his wages are quite low.
Forklift drivers don't earn much, and career progression
                tends to be slow.
But that's fine as long I have respect,
Which to be honest I don't, don't ever get.
Then he confesses and it's the final straw.
I don't accept society's messages anymore.
To change his ways, I will not beg.
I should have known when I saw the bulldog tattooed upon
                his leg.
So, he's gone, kicked to the kerb.
Suddenly life seems brighter, lighter,
Potentially quite superb.

You are a Mystery

You are a hidden cove on a deserted island.
You are beautiful but unfamiliar, and I don't know if I should
          stay.
You are a mystery, taking me down paths that lead back to
          the beginning.
Twisting paths of digits and letters that mess with my head.
You are a puzzle of shapes that whichever way I lay them do
          not fit together.
You are a 'choose your own adventure' story
and I am flitting from page to page urgently trying to save
          myself.
You are an unknown species, related but different, venom
          unknown.
But you are bright and enigmatic and I am drawn to you.
You are a mystery, an unsolved crime.
I suspect you, I accuse you in my mind, but I so want you to
          be innocent.
You are foreign food that I do not trust.
Foreign currency, that makes me feel vulnerable.
Foreign streets that lead to who knows where.
You make me feel like a blind man wandering across fields,
Yet I cannot stand still with you.
I try to read you in search of knowledge.
I study you in hope of learning.
I analyse you, try to interpret you.
I am desperate to know you, to understand your ways,

But you remain a mystery.

A beautiful magical mystery.

And the wonderful thing about mysteries is not knowing how they end.

Do You Love Me?

I ask you, 'do you love me?'
and you say, 'yes'.
I am trying to make my brain understand this truth,
It is backed up by overwhelming evidence,
It is obvious, it is reality,
It is a fact that you love me,
But my brain fights me like Big Daddy on a Saturday
          afternoon.
It thinks of a million reasons why this cannot be true,
It backs away like it has come across a monster,
Hides behind the curtains like a child at bedtime,
Refuses to hear the words, claims deafness,
Presents foolish stories to the contrary,
Tells me not to believe you,
That I am unlovable,
I have been sold a lie,
This is a scam,
A sales technique,
A woven web of deception,
It runs from your words, from your 3 little words,
It covers its ears,
Climbs a tree,
Hides underwater,
Goes to sleep,
Refuses to engage,
Chips away at my confidence, until I am forced to ask you

again,

'Do you love me?'

'Yes,' you reply.

But the file won't download,

The piece will not slot in,

The envelope does not fit,

The words jar,

They fade, ink faint on the page,

The book closes on itself,

She loves me?

The way is blocked,

The river flowing too fast to be crossed,

There are closures and diversions,

Until between ear and brain it gets completely lost and I
have to ask you once again,

'Do you love me?'

And again, you say, 'yes, I love you.'

But internal whispers state this is untrue.

The doubt creeps in, tiptoeing into my thoughts, stealing my
objectivity,

The voice will not be silenced,

It is screaming at me,

'SHE DOES NOT LOVE YOU!'

Too loud to not hear,

Too believable to ignore,

Why would she?

Why indeed?

It laughs at my optimism,

Sneers at my naivety,

Giggles at my romanticism, foolhardy, juvenile love until

finally, I shout,

'DO YOU REALLY LOVE ME?'

And you say,

'I will not say it again, what good are words?

I will live it every day until you are so loved your being
cannot deny love's existence,

Until you feel that love is the solid ground upon which you
stand,

Until my love has filled your soul, is brimming over,
drowning you in love,

Until you trust my love more than you trust yourself,

Until then,

Do not ask me, do I love you?

Just allow me to.'

In Residential

If I run and shout, swear and jump, leap and bounce will you
    freak out?
Will you say I'm bad, that I should control myself?
Will I make you sad or make you mad?
Will you lock me up if I wipe blood down your wall,
My distress painted for all to see?
The image of me in red, leaked and streaked across my bed.
If I talk in actions, will it be a distraction to your care?
Do you care?
About my nightmare?
And if you do,
Why do you not listen to the tears that glisten,
That sit beside my cuts and shouting,
That explode from me, when the anxiety is mounting?
Do you understand I cannot stop?
I'm rotting from within, the need to purge the urge to
    wound
The hope that then I'll be cocooned in someone's arms, but
    this is not the case.
Your shoulders sag, your fingers wag, pack my bag, move on.
You've probably forgotten me before I'm out the door,
Before my wounds have healed, are still so sore.
Do you understand what I'm about?
If I run and jump, leap and shout and swear,
Will you still care?
Does anyone care in Care?

One Night

Softly she spoke to me,
Moved confidently with purpose.
Her body firm, skin smooth muscles just bubbled beneath,
Her smile wide, her teeth white, her lips just right.
She flirted, laughed, and showed me what the future could be,
She spoke so eloquently.
Her brain so alive with ideas and stuff,
Stuff that I didn't know much about, not enough.
But she was mesmerising,
Almost prophesising that we should be together.
Promising that she would treat me like a princess,
'Yeah,' I thought and all the rest.
But there was something believable in her eyes,
Something about her that wasn't capable of lies.
We spent that evening talking on the rug.
Walking in the night something felt right.
A sensation I had never had before, not wanting to just be
                    cared for,
But a love that went straight to my very core.
I found myself believing in her,
My soul did concur,
My heart latched on,
And there will never be another one.
One night and now we are together,
One night that led to forever.

Chapter 2

Ecstasy and Elation

I remember that life was perfect, and I said to my boss at the time that I wanted to 'press pause, freeze time,' because everything was so good.

Work was amazing, my days were filled with time spent with amazing kids, I was part of an amazing team and I got paid for it. I felt young and free and confident.

I was hopelessly in love, living in Brighton and having a great time. We had wonderful holidays and went to lots of music gigs and had nights out at the theatre. Living in Brighton was exciting and vibrant.

I had never realised life and love could be so easy.

We Fit

Skin on skin, chin on chin, lips sync, eyes blink, moments
shared, souls bared,
Hearts that race, souls embraced, beat to the same drum,
I love you and I always will.
Time stands still, there's only one rule to this game, tell me
you feel the same.
I see your face, blood starts to race, there's no other, one
lover,
One match, no switch, set on fire, stars lit, perfect fit
Tell me what I need to hear, squash my fear, build me up, fill
my cup, get a ring, choose some bling, whatever
it takes, no mistake.
Wife strife, rest of life, sign me up, put down my name,
without blame,
Because I have no shame in feeling, reeling, believing you is
the one.
I'm gone, head heels, wheels in motion, too much emotion.
It's simple,
We fit and,
I love you.

Her Eyes

My love has eyes like toasted hazelnuts set in soft arches of
skin,
That once my eyes had met my heart would never forget
their gentle blink,
Which I will always return with a loving wink.
Her complexion is that of milky coffee,
Soft and smooth, with the sweetness of toffee.
A thousand smiles have left their trace,
Kindness evidenced upon her face.
Her expression contains more words than a million books
A glance conveys her heart in just one look and behind all
that lies a beautiful mind,
A constant whirring of worry, the injustice that jars,
The actions of people, that taints and mars her love of
humankind.
My love has eyes like creamy chocolate, floating in their
dinghies of skin.
Her complexion like barley.
Oh, my heart the top prize did win,
When it claimed her forever, my beautiful girl.

Wanting Her

My love is my preference, my want, my choice.
I do not need her warmth or her touch,
But I do desire it so much?

And if alone I will stand, I will rise, will not fall,
She is not my reason to breathe,
And yet I would beg her not to leave.

For life without her would be colourless and staid,
And I have become used to music and sunshine,
So, I would rather she remained mine.

And I hope that because she has the freedom to leave,
Knowing I will never stand in her way,
Somehow means she will stay.

And that out of a mutual wish to be together,
A wish to share laughter and fun,
We will grow old as one.

You Make me Feel

You make me feel like a hollyhock in summer, standing
               proud,
I can raise my head and be unashamed.
I nod in the wind, agreeing with the world.
In your presence I think differently, I move differently,
I am in water, smooth water, smooth warm water,
It keeps me afloat, keeps me moving, is gentle to my bones.
You make me feel that I am something special,
A vintage LP, a rare heirloom, something unique,
Something wonderful.
You make me feel I can get it wrong,
That perfection is not required.
You make me feel like I am lying on a grassy bank, cool
blades beneath me,
I am restful beside you,
The chaos in my head can stop,
Your presence turns the volume down.
You make me feel that I can trust,
That history is not a pattern, is not even a theme.
You make me believe that we are different, that we will
               always be different.
I am in a tunnel of you, too narrow to turn around, no need
             to see behind.
With you the rain is just a backdrop, we are cosy indoors,
With you the thunder is classical music,
With you I know that the storm cannot shake me,

I can dance without care, without inhibition,
run free and be happy.

What a Shame

Perfect nails, perfect hair, eyebrows perfect pair.
Mind got skewed as she looked in the mirror,
No love, no glimmer, just wishes she was slimmer,
Self-hate no debate in fact, it's a family trait.
Compliments on screen but some are mean,
They stick as she flicks over the page, her stage.
Words hurt, call her dirty, ugly, fat, chop off your head you'd
        be better off dead.
One guy starts to chat, says, 'you ain't all that but let's see
        you without that top.'
She types, "Stop."
But she lies in bed at night knows he's right,
She'll do it and maybe he'll be her man.
She's got a plan, post a picture #wantsex,
Webcam on she sends a text,
He replies, 'let's see your breasts,' then says; 'I wanna see the
        rest.'
Her ego stroked, she feels real stoked,
She strikes a pose.
Image he posts and boasts that she's his girl.
Her tits are hits with his mates,
They rate her high, he says they're going out
She pouts, but doubts,
Doesn't want do today but must obey or he'll say goodbye.
She gives the pics, he saves the clips and sends them round
        the world,

They'll never disappear let's be clear when she's old and wise
she'll despise the things she did but she won't
ever get rid,

Potential bosses giggle as she wriggles in her chair,

They say no because of what they see for free.

They frown she says she can't take them down.

She begs them to be kind, but they think she's dirty, far too
flirty,

A big grey cloud that follows her around.

If only she could go back in time, tell herself she's fine and
help her love herself.

What she wouldn't give to live that time again with her head
screwed on,

He'd be gone, no threats, regrets or shame.

What a shame.

Closer

It is not enough to be close to you.
It is not enough to hold you or lie next to you.
I want to be a part of you, ingrained in you.
I want your body to envelop me and cover me.
I want to climb into you and rest against your lungs.
I want to be stirred into you, like sugar into tea.
Blended into you like an onion into soup, attached to you
        like a skin graft.
I want to be etched into you.
I want to be a permanent mark upon you, like ink tattooed.
I want to be a drug injected into your system, blood
        transfused into your veins.
I want to calcify on your bones, plant my roots like a strand
        of hair into your head.
I want to be released like serotonin into your brain.
I want to hang out behind your eyes and see what you see.
I want to climb up your rib cage and be deafened by the
        sound of your heartbeat.
I want to play piano on your teeth and strum your fringe like
        the strings of a guitar.
I want to peek out from behind your eyelashes and slide
        down your nose.
Then, I want to lie in the curve of your ear and listen to the
        gentle lullaby of your breathing,
Rocked by the rise and fall of your chest,
I want to fall asleep in you.

The Allotment of Love

Our love grows tomato red and beetroot purple, deep and
earthy,
Has grown from a small pale bean that barely knew this
world.
Was sowed in deep soil and nurtured every day,
From tiny seed, a buried fleck to an abundant harvest.
We have worked at the ground that was rubble and sand,
Been patient with each other and enriched the land.
Love that has grown like potatoes with reaching tubers
taking more territory.
Stems with leaves bursting and uncurling, growing wider
and taller.
Raspberry canes heavy with berries that reach and stretch up,
Luscious leaves that shine so bright, that take light and make
it into growth.
Flowers, with petals of pink and white, daisy chains and
fields of four-leaf clover.
New species of roses where butterflies go to inhale the scent,
Buttercups that make your skin glow.
Our love is not a seed or bulb, not fruit or vegetable,
It is not plant or shrub or tree,
It is a whole allotment that blossoms with love,
Grown by you and me.

Keep the Love (my love)

I'm lucky, blessed for all I've confessed, you still love me.
I never thought it could be this good,
But I'm in it.
Sparks fly.
Content, every promise meant.
I'm not wealthy, healthy, clever or that together, but you saw
            something good.
I'm not the brightest, lightest, no medals, awards, no fame,
            just shame.
I'm shy,
I cry,
Because the past lasts.
Honesty a must, you saw you could trust that I was real,
I feel,
And it's out there like glass.
No mask,
Nothing hidden,
You care,
We share,
Wear our hearts on our sleeves.
One pair of lives intertwined,
Mashed up, merged, blurred into,
One life that is,
So,
Very,
Beautiful.

I love your open heart,
Your willingness to impart how you feel about me.
I love that you love me.
Others split, love quit,
But I know you'll stay mine.
We give the other what they need to hold on,
In body and emotion, no commotion, no drama.
It's calmer, my soul can rest with,
My,
Best,
Friend.

We lean on each other,
I read your face,
Expect your grace.
I don't feel good enough, but I guess that's just tough.
I've learnt not to question your love,
My love.
Stay here forever together,
In the love we've created,
Unabated, pouring, roaring, robust, trust.
We must never let go,
Keep the love,
My love.

Those Eyes

Big eyes,
Big brown eyes,
Eyes that see far more than most,
Eyes that read looks and body language,
Tiny little movements do not escape those eyes.
Those eyes are like sensors, bomb detectors,
Tuned into you,
They don't just see,
They know.
They know what it means,
When you twitch, when you scratch,
If a dimple appears,
A crease or a wrinkle.
Those eyes that blink,
That deny any wrongdoing,
That beg, that stare,
That communicate so effectively,
That desire love,
Indicate affection,
Pain and rejection.
Those eyes that watch you,
Follow you,
Never leave you.
Sometimes those eyes are defiant,
Wilful, disobedient,
Glaring, disbelieving.

Eyes that turn away.
Those eyes,
That shut gently with pleasure,
But are always ready,
That are never quite closed.
Soft eyelashes that move with dreams,
That only those eyes see.
I love those eyes,
Those deep brown,
Dachshund eyes.

Clubbing

Dance, throw your feet to the left, your arms in the air,
Throw shapes without thought or care,
Move and bounce to the beat.
Jump as high as you can and land on your feet,
Twirl in the sky, leap so you fly,
Slide along the floor, then do it all some more.
Flick your hair around,
Body pop, hit the ground,
Listen to the rhythm, listen to the sound,
Let it get into your ears, let it pound.
Move in synch, don't stop, don't blink,
Move in time, open mouth, lyrics mime.
Don't say it's the end of the night,
Please, don't turn on the light.
Legs suddenly like lead,
Sounds ringing in my head,
Room spins,
Unsteady on my pins,
Feel sick, groan,
Try to get a taxi home.
There is a terrible pain in my head,
'What a great night.' you said.
I think tomorrow,
I will stay in my bed.

Chapter 3

When the Sky Falls In

I miss Mark, he was a very special person, so incredibly beautiful. I am still connected to him through his three gorgeous children, whom I love dearly, and he certainly lives on in them.

Mark took me for a coffee when I found out I had Parkinson's. He insisted on getting me out of the house, despite my protests that I wanted to stay under my duvet. We entered the restaurant, and he asked the waiter if they had a table near the toilets as I might need it at short notice. He laughed as I smiled through my tears for the first time since receiving the diagnosis. I am just sad he's not around still, I kind of need him.

I have been lucky enough to find a partner who is loyal and committed, incredibly loving, ferociously protective, and my best friend. True love is not hard work, it does not require compromise, because when you love each other, you always want the best for each other.

I like writing love poems; they are the most natural thing for me to create.

Finding out I had Parkinson's was tough, but I had two choices, give up or get on and I chose to get on. I have to renew that commitment every day. Some days I do feel like giving up, but I can't. There is too much good stuff still out there to experience.

The End of Something Beautiful

It's a nursing home, not your home,
But it's where you live,
Where your life will end, my beautiful friend.
Behind the door I know that there will be less of you than
           before,
Less of the man I love and more of the cancer that has bored
           into your body,
Cruelly crept and crawled, its cells sprawled deep into your
           being,
That it has no right to infiltrate but it is stateless,
Alien invader.
I hate its existence, its disrespect of your persistence to live.
You are in bed, your head so much bigger than the rest of you.
Soon you will disappear,
My fear that you will disintegrate to dust.
I touch you while there is still something solid,
Wafer thin skin,
Wrinkled and crinkled but you are still in there.
I run my fingers through your hair and stare into your eyes,
which slowly open.
Our friendship is beautifully connected, cannot be
interrupted, interjected.
My feeling is perfectly reflected by your smile.
We spend happy moments together; no cancer cells can
steal.

You are living, real, heart beating, mind whirring, ideas
              stirring, currently occurring,
You are still my friend,
I will be here at the end.

You were so calm, so dignified when you died.
I watched the sunset and let go.

Wheelies and Glo-sticks

I'm wheelies and glo-sticks not wheelchairs and walking
        sticks.
The pile of daily pills gets larger when the only drugs I took
        before were B&H White and too much lager.
I bounce, I run, I'm dodging in and out,
Life's a blast, lived fast.
I don't wait for no one, but now somehow, I'm too slow,
Whose hands are these?
Someone's shaky mitts that won't comply.
Legs that drag,
I can't stop this limp,
Limbs on the blink.
My body's broke.
Words spoken won't sink in.
I think they got it wrong see, coz I'm wheelies and glo-sticks,
        not wheelchairs and walking sticks.

I compete, no feat too hard,
I play, I stay to the bitter end,
Never quit, I don't sit,
Rest is for the weak, but I'm tired.
I can't stay, can't even stand today,
Can't take part, can't even get to the start.
Who is this freak who needs her sleep?
I think they got it wrong see, coz I'm wheelies and glo-sticks,
        not wheelchairs and walking sticks.

I'm a fighter, all-nighter, love clubs and booze,
Nothing to lose.
Last one to bed, rise with a clear head,
Party on, get stuff done,
Going here, there and everywhere,
But I'm not strong.
I long for my pillow.
Will I ever feel right?
Muscles tight, cramps and spasms,
A massive chasm is growing between who I was and who I am.
I think they made an error.
Don't they know?
I'm wheelies and glo-sticks, not wheelchairs and walking
          sticks.

Dance with Me

Dance with me before my legs give in,
Dance with me one last time, so I can feel free.
I will be like paper in the wind, like rubbish in a storm,
I will be free.
I hope the music won't ever stop.
Dance with me in the kitchen or on the lawn,
Dance with me whilst we still can, so I can feel weightless,
I will be like a fish that moves with ease, like a dragonfly in
            spring.
I will fly.
I will keep on moving because it makes me forget.
Dance with me before it is too late,
Dance with me in your arms, so I'll know I'm alive,
I will be like smoke in the sky, like a flame that flickers,
I will be beautiful.
I will dance because it makes me feel young.
Dance with me,
While I can still dance.

Travelling

I never want to walk anywhere with you,
I want us to hover above the ground, levitate and glide,
I want us to hang onto the wings of a butterfly and take the
        slow train of a worm.
I want us to leap from a cliff with the lemmings and slide
        down the rabbit hole.
I want us to travel through the mole's tunnel and sit in the
        swallow's nest.
I want us to ride unicorns over the mountains to where the
        wise man lives in a magical forest.
I want us to fall to the ground in the lid of an acorn, or swirl
        down on its helicopter leaf.
When we land, we will be carried off by the claws of an eagle
        that will puncture through our clothes and take
        us up into the skies, into the blue, into the white
        foam of a cloud.
When that bird has taken us further than the cruise ships
        below have travelled in weeks, we will take off
        our jackets and plunge into the ocean.
Seahorses will blink as we unsettle the sand where they rest
        and sharks will turn on a sixpence at our arrival.
We will dance with seaweed in our hair to the backdrop of a
        thousand neon creatures, under the spotlights of
        jellyfish.
We will line dance with an octopus and be transported by a
        sideways stepping crab.

We will hold on to his antennae and steer him
                      toward a sea urchin that shines luminesce
Caught up in a mackerel shoal we will dart through the sea
              with a deep sense of belonging, until we are
              dumped on the deck of a fisherman's trawler
Caught in the nets
Time to rest and let the little boat carry us home.

I Don't Want to Live Without You

I do not want to live without you.
My bed would feel cavernous without you in it,
The night would feel threatening but in the day time I would
feel exposed and want to hide.
In fact, I would always want to hide, want to be hidden.
If you left me, my heart would become hard like stone, it
would close and seal itself like a diver's bell.
My lungs would not pump air if it did not smell of you.
My stomach would refuse food we had not shared.
My eyes would not open for the fear of seeing nothing.
My mind would become confused by your absence and reject
this reality.
Without you I would rot, dark mould appearing, to indicate I
am perished.
I would shut down.
I would rust from the acidity of your
abandonment and this would spread throughout
me until I disintegrate.
I would be covered in holes, spaces left by you, punctured by
your leaving, punched into my body by your lack
of reciprocation.
People would see through me and pity me.
They would look at my transparency and notice my swollen,
infected heart and shake their heads.
My heart would be inflamed and sore, my soul collapsed, my

       spine crumbled.

No one would be able to save me, no surgery would be able
       to stem the internal bleeding.

No bandage could wrap itself around a loss so big, no drugs
       could calm my breathing.

My arms would not bend without being loosened by your
       affection.

My legs would not hold me up without your face to rise to.

I would never love another.

Stay with me.

I don't want to ever live without you.

I Miss You

As the salmon's lungs burst and burn with desperation,
As his stretched heart feels the reality of swimming
upstream,
So, my heart bursts without you.
As it forces itself to believe that it is possible, that the top is
within its reach,
So, I force myself to hope that your return is not a fanciful
whim, but is written in fate.
Just as the salmon knows in his scaly head that some will
survive,
'Why not me?' he says, and I will say the same.
As God chooses the salmon that will make it to their
destination,
So, I will hope that you will choose me.
Just as the great fish faces death but will not stop,
So, I would rather face death than lose you forever.
I miss you and as nature intended for the fish to die or not
and the eggs to be laid or not,
So, I will believe that nature intended us to be one.
I am strong for you my love.
I will swim upstream to get to you my love.
When I get there, when I collapse without breath in my body,
I will lie on the riverbed looking up at the sky and hope that
your face will fill the space and peer down upon
me.
Until then, I miss you.

The Benefit of Love

I propose a change to the welfare system,
Entitling us all to the benefit of love.
So, love becomes a right and not a privilege.
Public love services not private love care,
Universal love not universal credit,
Personal love payments and family love top ups.
Not bread queues but love queues.
Protesters with placards that read 'we want love,'
'No more poverty,' replaced with,' no more hate.'
Crimes of love and love rehabilitation.
Youngsters claiming parental love where they have none.
Single person love allowances.
Not children's homes, loving homes.
Loveless marriages transformed by state handouts.
Old age reinvigorated by annuities of love.
Schools teaching love and hospitals mending broken hearts.
MPs fighting for love in their constituencies.
Manifestos based on love rates not tax rates.
Affection rates high.
People sharing and supporting.
Loving their neighbours.
No barriers to love.
A country rich in love.
Whose identity is love.
No national anthem just a love anthem.
So much love for every person,

From the cradle to the grave.
Wouldn't we all benefit
From the benefit of love?

Victoria Station

Your face so soothing, smiling at me in a sea of strangers.
The comfort of your body as you greet me.
Your warmth against me in a crowd of a hundred frozen
        souls.
Your hands that take me, lead me, show me the way,
Guide me out of the throng of so many lost creatures,
Creatures that scurry and hurry not knowing which way
        happiness is.
Your feet that walk beside mine are in sync with me,
Click to clack in harmony.
Steps taken together, in a population infected with
        loneliness.
Your thoughts that think not of yourself, ensure protection
        for me physically,
Looking out always watching.
Your heart that beats with mine, tuned in,
That will care for every particle of my being,
That will love me in a loveless society.
Thank you for being here to meet me,
At Victoria Station.

Chapter 4

Life Looks Different

My mother-in-law gave me a beautiful ring, which was given to her by her husband, my late father - in - law. She of course gave it to me with his blessing. It is my most prized possession and has enormous meaning. When my father-in-law died, it was unbelievably sad. He really was the most incredible, intelligent, capable, and loving gentleman.

I don't know which has been harder, adjusting to life with Parkinson's or life without 'Daddy'. The poem Daddy was written for my partner who has found life without him extremely painful.

Also, an existing friendship has intensified. She has mental health problems. I don't care. She is a wonderful, uplifting, caring and hilariously funny person.

The Ring

The ring that sings of many things has gold and stone but it
              comes from heartbroken bone.
It sings of love and thoughts of our own mortality.
Give, live, watch the joy,
Through tears, fears fade, thoughts weighed, sits nice, glows
              bright and is so right in time.
A sign of love, of fitting in and being part of kin.
She sees the ring, she feels it's meant, a loving vent,
Words drift, brains sift and forget with regret but the ring
              that sings will never lose its sheen, stop being seen.
Will always shine bright with its light and gold and its
              message bold,
Onto which she'll hold,
Forever.

Some Days

Down days with a low gaze
The future plays upon my mind
My heart can't lift itself today
I cower, I sleep under my duvet

Alive days with steely glaze
In this phase I'm going to win
I am the strongest
These days are the happiest, the longest

No days are without thought
I have fought, but it is like a shadow
It's now residing in its lair
In my brain, its home is there

Some days when I think
My fears link and infiltrate my soul
I worry, it feels like fate
That me it will obliterate

Acceptance days with eyebrows raised
I say, I'm not fazed by you
I can rise above it
I tell it to be quiet and just sit

Hopeful days, a cure will come
I feel the lure of belief that it could
Then my heart will sing
Until then, what will tomorrow bring?

Daddy

I sit and wonder where he is, where did he go from here?
How could he consume my life my heart and then simply
        disappear?
Why do I see him everywhere when my eyes are shut or
        open?
How come I hear his voice, his words so softly spoken?
How can my heart be so full of love even though my heart is
        broken?
He is still in everything I do or think or say,
And yet he is nowhere,
He's still gone as the dawn brings each new day.
Does he know how much he's missed, what a hole he's left?
Does he see my tears, my sadness, my lack of sleep or rest?
Will he still be proud of me when I do something well?
Will he still smile when I have some news to tell?
I just don't understand where my Daddy's gone,
When he was so healthy, so very big and strong.
I don't understand how God wouldn't know that I need him
        More,
That I need every inch of him, every bone, every muscle,
        every pore.
Why did he go?
I'll never know.
I'll never stop loving him.
But God please help me heal my heart,
Don't let this sadness win.

Help me be brave and strong, just like he showed me how to.
Help me reflect his goodness in everything I do.

What if Love?

What if love showed itself on people like rolls of fat that
gather and bulge?
What if love spewed over the top of your jeans like a thick
waisted middle-aged man,
Dribbled down your sides and gathered in puddles at your
feet like an overfilled pint?
What if love showed like gold jewellery on a gangster,
glimmering and shining for everyone to see his
wealth,
Love falling off in great globules, like a lavish scone with too
much cream and jam?
What if skinny people were pitied for their loveless
existence?
Surgeons performing love adding operations.
Collagen injections adding love to your lips.
Fat people blossoming like cherry trees in spring, like snow
blizzards in winter.
Love falling on them, layer after layer of big fat love.
People so in love they can't get through the door.
Can't walk because their loved filled thighs rub together,
chafing and burning with love.
Fat feet planted in love.
Fat hands caressing a lover.
Fats knees aching under the pressure of too much love.
Chubby children loved by their parents.
Chunky do-gooders getting fatter by the day.

Walking down the street glancing at other fat ones, nodding
        to them smugly.
Love dripping off them all like beads of sweat.
Big fat love on your big fat face.
Love breaking out in pimples and spots, filled with liquid
        love.
Breaking through skin particles and hair follicles,
Making great love lumps all over your body.
Taking over your physical self until you explode with love,
        internally combust.
Love flying everywhere,
Landing on pedestrians,
Licked up by stray dogs,
Carried off by hungry birds,
Inhaled by an open mouth jogger,
Splattered onto the windscreen of a passing car,
A love shower raining down.
What if you are just another loved life,
Bursting and disappearing,
Leaving nothing but a legacy of love,
That drifts off on the wind?

I am Colour

I am yellow, cowardly custard, yet keen as mustard.
A little bit of sunshine, a weed but a nice one like a
dandelion.
I am blue, some days I get quite down.
Other days I am as high as the sky and I fly.
There are so many shades of blue, I love navy and turquoise
        too.
I am green, like peas or grass, or trees.
Green can be sickening but I think as a colour it's just fine.
I am friendly but cross me, and I'll be prickly like pine.
Uneducated yet bright, perhaps I am lime.
I am black, I am night, nocturnal.
Creative in the early hours,
This is when my brain flowers, blooms with ideas, of the
        night I have no fears.
I am red, aim for victory,
Outrageous and enraged,
I do not turn the page or let go without the last word, I am
        pillar box red, head strong.
I am white.
Fluffy and soft, I give in.
Can be deflated with a pin.
White, that can be missed, can be just mist.
I am pink, I am in party mode,
I like to celebrate in style,
But I haven't done so for a while.

I am a rainbow.
A mix of shade and light, a palette of paint,
That changes as you wait.
I am splashes and sploshes of colour,
A wonder, a sight to behold.
Fold into the paper,
The colours recede as I sleep,
Black and white,
Until later.

Inside You

If I opened you up what would be inside?
A million tiny hearts lit up like fairy lights, pegged to your
soul.
A pink striped paper bag of sherbet lemons for a liver and a
quarter pound of wine gums for a kidney.
Your brain glowing neon, like a New York theatre sign
advertising your incredible thoughts.
Bones of Kendal Mint Cake.
Smooth blended coffee flowing beneath your skin.
Rivers of coffee that carry a trillion minuscule ships each
bearing cargos of knowledge that travel within
you.
Landing at the port of your mind and unloading into your
mouth behind which hides the smiles of a
thousand small children, giggling and laughing as
they push up the corners of your lips.
If I opened you up, a billion small fairies would fly from your
lungs,
Fiery sparks shooting from their paper-thin wings
sprinkling magic dust as they go.
Lungs made from white marshmallows, pumping not air but
perfume with such a sweet scent, blackcurrant
with hints of vanilla.
If I opened you up the brightness would be blinding, the
power of you enough to knock me off my feet.
It would be magical and wonderous and amazing.

It would be like opening a treasure trove, releasing a wild
        animal,
Shooting rockets into space, making DNA.
But I don't need to see inside you,
I know what exists beneath your skin.

The Map of You

Head first, just like I dive into you,
Hair that shines, light reflected, smooth and sleek like the
shell of a fresh hazelnut.
Below sit the whirls of delight that give you sight,
Sweet eyes upon which lashes sit and ponder.
I wonder if they know that the face where they rest is so
loved?
Your nose not upwards in the air, has a humble forward
stare.
Straight lines running down to lips that have small creases,
your history of smiles and wails, success, failure,
good and happy times marked into your skin,
You smile most when you win.
Lines that defy time, you defy time, and you win a lot.
Your chin is strong and set, aligned with body and mind,
Neck leads to shoulders square, shoulders that bear the
burdens of others, lovers and mothers that push
against the wind and stand up to blows of sorrow
yesterday, today and tomorrow.
Shoulders upon which I stand because without which I
would fall, but, instead,
I land in your beautiful lap, like this body was planned to
hold me up.
Your contours guide me, show me the way,
The map of you is what I follow,
The journey upon which I decide each day to go,

Within the folds of which I lay,
The landscape I chose to live in,
The place I reside within.
The map of you with oceans of blue and valleys and fields,
A treasure map of hidden gold.
I am the only one told where to find it and I have marked it
            with a cross.
And if I lost you, I would search forever, seek and not rest,
I would dedicate my life to finding you and when I do,
I would stake my claim upon your chest.

The Sea

Smoky seas that breathe and sigh
That swell with the tides and lunar cycles
That house a million creatures of every size
That sit below and, on the surface
The surface that the sparks dance upon
Uncatchable is the sun's glitter
Seagulls weave overhead, float above
Below the ripple the endless depth that belies the brain
That provides its own light and shade
The whales that glide silently
Twisting seals that pop up occasionally
The sea's tousled ends push into land
And the only sign it's been there is the seaweed abandoned
Green ribbons left upon the darkened sand

I Choose You

Trauma in your body stored,
Marked on your skin, programmed your brain.
Physical reactions make you believe that you're insane.
Always watching, looking out,
You doubt that you're okay.
Today you wonder, ponder on your mind,
You find that it's confused, bemused.
You are not amused by the chaos and bombardment,
The self-hatred which the truth has bent.
Negativity that's never spent,
Overwhelms you with fear.
Detaching from the world,
Helps avoid hurled messages that come constantly.
Do you know that despite your battle with yourself,
You are wonderful, despite your mental health?
You have wealth in so many ways.
You are not the problem.
I am not fazed.
From the past these issues stem, from nasty men,
From all the bad things done to you,
As a little girl without love you grew,
Trauma stuck like glue upon your being.
I wish that I could wash it away,
Keep all of your demons firmly at bay.
But I know it's not simple or quick,
This trauma will take time to unstick,

But I do think,
That, however mad you think you might be,
There's no other friend I'd choose for me.

Chapter 5

A Different Pain

I never knew what 'pain' was until I had a prolapsed disc, which was pressing on my nerves. I do not have the words to explain how much it hurt. The experience also humbled me greatly. I was completely dependent on strangers to do everything for me. I very quickly had to get over my pride and any embarrassment.

It was a double-edged sword. I felt horrendous, I cried with the pain and begged the nurses to make it stop but, at the same time, I saw the wonderful kindness of human beings. There were some very special nurses and doctors that spent time listening to me and understanding my fears, even when their shift was over some time ago.

The most joyous day was leaving hospital and going home to my beautiful life.

I also realised I am stronger than I think.

I've Never Felt so Fragile

I've never felt so fragile, never felt like glass,
I was solid, concrete, waterproof, travelled fairly fast.
I've never felt like china, limbs that move so slow,
Legs that feel like lead, feet that just won't go.
Bones that might break, fear so very great,
Lifting each foot in an anxious state.
Nerve pains won't go away,
They won't today.
Lacking in patience, time ticking on,
Gone is my confidence, my stride.
I can confide in friends,
That I worry how this ends.
I don't think I'm bomb proof any more,
I'm fragile, vulnerable, raw.
I'm beat up, battered and sore.
I might be okay again,
I just don't know when.
I am made of spider web, gently strung, hung on a tree.
Amongst the fear let's make it clear,
I have hope, will cope,
Will try my best to rest and believe,
Relieve the fear, find another gear,
Try my best to make myself metal, hard and strong.
I long for it, to feel fit.
What I desire I will fight for,
Imagine myself with an iron core,

More and more layers to make it tough,
Until it's not fragile, there's enough,
For me to not feel like a spider's web anymore.
Store that feeling and keep believing,
You'll not be fragile forever,
You're an iron bar not a feather.
I know this in my heart.
From brain to body, I must impart.
It will heal,
Because this fragility is temporary, unreal,
Not a permanent state.
This is not my story, not my fate.
I'm not made of glass, I am resilient, bold.
I'm made of brick, of leather,
I am made of solid gold.

Where is Heaven?

Where is Heaven?
Heaven is far up high.
I know this because people always point to the sky when
    they say it.
It is the willow tree on the riverbank when your eyes require
    a beautiful scene.
It is knowing when winter has come by the sight of your
    breath and the crunch beneath your feet of a pine
    cone.
It is knowing that when I get in,
You'll be home.

Without You

I walk along the water's edge, but the river does not flow the
same way without you.
The litter that bobs along on the surface, travelling so fast is
like little pieces of you disappearing from reach.
The urge to jump in and salvage those pieces, those
fragments of your being is overwhelming.
I reason with myself they are not you.
A swan bends its neck contorting itself into a heart.
I look around and see pairs, twos, men and women meant
for one another, walking arm in arm.
The sight of them, their intimacy, him giving her his scarf,
her nuzzling into his jacket is like claws tearing into my
flesh.
Love is everywhere, I shield my eyes from it.
I turn around, away from the water and the love infected
couples.
I turn to the road where the buses pull in and the taxis pull
out,
But I see your face in every window and I see you waiting at
the stop.
I run across the road, cars beeping and burning rubber as
they brake.
When I reach the little covered shelter, the bus slows but
there is no one, just an old lady in a green
mackintosh who flashes her card and hobbles
up the steps, the doors close behind her,

With drivers still waving fists at me I leave and follow the
pavement home.
I pass youngsters with headphones, and they are laughing at
me.
I pass an old man shuffling along, a roll up sat upon his lip,
which is curled in a sneer because he is mocking
me.
Somehow, they know you left.
They laugh at my unrequited love, my abandonment.
I will get home and it will be cold, even with the sun's
warmth, it will be cold.
There will be sound, but it will be meaningless.
There will be colour, but my eyes will dull it.
There is no life without you in it.
My heart breaks with solitude, is broken, cracked, splintered,
smashed into a thousand fragments,
Is like grains of sand that rush through my fingers and can
never be put back together.
I get to the front door and you open it before I can reach my
key.
'Where have you been?' you ask, kissing my cheek.
'Just for a walk,' I say.
'Why are you crying?' you ask.
'I was just imagining life without you,' I reply before opening
my arms which you require no invitation to enter.
I breathe again.

Wash it Off

I want to wash it off my skin.
The stench that will not leave, weaves its way into my
        nostrils, lingers,
The fingers pressing into me, needles invading, pervading
        my sense of autonomy,
I am but one of many.
The feelings that have crept upon me,
The weakness I don't want me to be,
The taste that fills my mouth and stays on my tongue,
The old people that do not make me look young,
The many sounds of carrying and fetching, blood pressure
machines and retching,
Trolley wheels, nurses' heels squeaking on tiled corridors,
Humans leaking life and hope, crying that they just can't
        cope.
I need to get out of here.
Oppression, pain and thick black fear.
I need to brush it off my teeth,
Remove it from my hair,
Wipe it from my brow, how does it pervade me so.
What type of place is this that leaves its mark,
Is restoring me and is yet so dark?
This hospital with all its smells and sound,
That around my fragile brain are wound.
Now I'm out I never want to return to there,
For all its brilliance and its care,

I will leave here and enter into the light of home,
The familiar spaces I used to roam,
And all this will drain away, fade into just memory.
For surely the key to my recovery,
Where this experience of hospital will be finally shed,
Will be at home where I can sleep in my own bed.

Pocket Love

When you are not with me, I know that I carry your love
Before I leave, you slip it into my pocket
Like my guardian angel keeping me safe
I feel you there against my thigh
Your love warm against my skin
You are present, so close to me
I can almost feel your heartbeat through my clothes
You nudge me, poke me when I lose faith
You knock against me when my confidence wanes
I can hear you gently singing in synch with my stride
Humming contentedly from your hiding place
I am never alone, never away from you
Because your love fits so perfectly into my pocket

Everywhere is Yellow

Everywhere is yellow.
Like breakfast cereal,
Cornflake colour.
The land is crisp and dry,
The sun has taken all the green,
Has sucked out all the bright,
And left this blanched, sun scorched landscape.
I feel the crunch beneath my feet,
Where once was grass that folded,
Damp between my toes,
Now it snaps, crackles and pops.
Where once the leaves were dark and lush,
Now they are brown toast.
Bran flakes fallen to the ground.
The garden lawns, the roadsides,
The parks and public spaces look like margarine spread
                    across my bread.
The sun a great big egg with albumen clouds,
That is too big for my egg cup,
But maybe God will eat it up.
People lying on the beach,
Turning over like rashers of bacon on the grill,
Fat people with perfect tanned bellies like cooked sausages.
I wonder what will happen if the sun remains,
And breakfast ends,
What comes after yellow?

Holding on

Holding onto you, a string from your heart held tightly,
You lift me like you are made from helium.
Gripping your love, clawing into the dirt to ensure you stay,
Scrabbling against rockfall, feet slipping,
Constantly adjusting, trying to please.
I am unsure of the knot that we tied,
Scared it will fray, slip, be gnawed by small creatures,
Conspiring in corners,
Scared it will not hold the weight of our burdens, our fears.
Yet you are my safety net,
My lifeboat, my parachute.
On you I float, swing, fling myself on your mercy.
I am trying to hold on, will not let you go.
Fasten myself with Velcro, I will stick it with glue,
Zip up, fasten tight, because I cannot hold on without you.

A Painting Called Peace

I play with wire and clay, I mould and bend and flex stuff.
I make pictures with oil and spray paint, liquid ink,
I write in pen, on screen I craft words to be heard and seen,
Poetry to convey emotion, sometimes cause some thought
        commotion.
I am going to change and take a paint brush to myself,
Switch my physical being for the canvas,
Mark it with a new me,
Brushstrokes that I want to be,
Sculpt my body and my brain,
Create some goodness, release its pain,
Sketches in pencil and charcoal,
Soft shading to make the picture whole,
Spray myself neon pink,
Highlight the thoughts I ought to think,
Build this body strong like a model kit,
The broken bits I'll stick back on, varnish with care,
I'll strip it back until it's bare,
Until I can see what parts of me need the rust removing,
Some oil and sandpaper for a mind that needs some gentle
        soothing,
Find a way to upgrade outdated, inefficient limbs,
Nurture them and give them time, make them feel again like
        mine.
Make myself a Michelangelo,
A portrait of perfection.

Colours that will flow,
I'm thinking O'Keefe, Monet, Matisse, a painting I'll call
'Peace.'
Tones that do not jar but sit together,
Slotted sections, dovetail joints, the finished work that
points to a labour of love.
A work of art that people see as fine, a masterpiece,
physically mine.
From this darkness where I lurk, comes a new beginning,
A belief that over this physically I can win,
A pledge to embrace it and own it, let it be,
A commitment that my new life's work, this piece of art,
Will be me.

Chapter 6

Reflections and Forward Momentum

When you have been lying on your back for four weeks, unable to move, you do a lot of reflecting. I decided in that time, I need to take better care of myself (hence 'A Painting Called Peace'). I realised that although I had accepted and, in many ways, come to terms with my diagnosis of Parkinson's, I hadn't accepted that this means I need to make some lifestyle changes. I am not normal, and I can't do everything I used to. That's not being negative, I can do things, I just must accept I get tired, get stiff muscles and have to factor in things like rest and recovery.

I also realised what a great bunch of friends I have. They visited me in hospital and at home, rang me incessantly and sent me cards and flowers and all sorts of gifts. I would look forward to visiting hours with such anticipation and those hours flew.

My family were also incredible.

I have a wonderful relationship and a very happy life. I am content and in times of pain this contentment helps me ride the storms and dance through the rain.

I love and am loved...What more can I ask for?

You Are No Longer a Mystery

Your love for me is an enigma no more.
I figure after 17 years together we are pretty set and I should
        stop being insecure.
Everything we are, everything we stand for
Is good and beautiful.
We have been blessed by this messy love,
Punctuated by tragedy, dented by loss, at times in pain,
But love has never wavered, never waned,
Always remained the same.
We grip each other on this white-knuckle ride,
Wait until the tide turns,
Which like sunrise it always will.
There are no words that describe my love for you,
I wish there were,
I could say it in every language known to man, yet it cannot
        translate,
Can't explain how you permeate my soul.
Your love is no longer an enigma, no longer a mystery to be
        solved.
I just need to be me because that's who you fell in love with
        despite my imperfections.
I realise it is simple,
Our love is true.
I feel so happy when I see you,
There is no shade only bright sunlight that does not fade.
You love me,

I love you back and we bask in the wealth of this wondrous
thing we have,
That has infected every pore of us,
Has become the very core of who we are,
Your love is a mystery no more.

One Eye

I look into your eye.
I see the centre, black like a full stop, with a tiny window of
        light in the corner.
This is the bit I imagine I can climb into and take a twisting
        slide all the way to your soul.
The light reflects the chestnut brown of your iris, shines
        outward.
 I can see you are smiling just from the sparkle that you emit.
There are little squiggles surrounding your colour,
Blending together like marble, like marbled water,
I fantasise about swimming in this marble pool.
I would dive deep down and find the very bottom of your
        eyeball.
That pool darkens at the rim, making your beautiful eye
        stand out,
Highlighted by a thin black border.
Your lashes waver overhead, fluttering, keeping order,
Tiny limbs that sway above, pointing with their fingers to
        your eye,
Sign posting the world to this exquisite location.
That eye sees me, rests in motion,
I know, because I am a printed image on it,
Transferred, tattooed into your sight.
A mighty vision of love.
If your eye could see further, beyond my skin it would see
        that this love is also embedded in my heart,

Tiny veins part, allowing me into muscle and there, buried
                    beneath tissue, is you.
You are my very heartbeat.
Your eye blinks and then re-establishes contact with my face,
I have to stop staring at your eye, let go of this special place,
I leave but remain imprinted there.
Your eye will always wear that picture, a photo of me.
When it comes to love,
I hope I am all you see.

The Reluctant Poet

I write, and I write, and I write,
I bleed poems, bruise in words, have wounds from rhyme
            and scabs from lines.
I am a reluctant poet,
Poetry falls off me, just constantly
            comes into my brain drives me insane.
There are so many,
They tumble out,
Waterfalls of words and I have to herd them into sentences,
Make sense of what is in my head.
I have to formulate some paragraphs that give justice to the
            letters.
I will write into the night without sight of anyone, through
            the wee hours,
Until dawn flowers again, when I will still be with my pen,
Making marks upon the paper,
When morning comes and it can't get any later.
How can I stop when the words keep popping out?
In my mind they are sometimes a whisper,
Sometimes a shout,
But there is rarely nothing, they are never silent.
I never get a blank brain.
The days are all the same,
One big word game,
How many can we write today?
It's actually quite tedious for me,

Sometimes I feel I'm experiencing death by poetry.
And my poor family, suffering similes and analogies,
The emotion, the description and the tone,
This poetry should leave us all alone.
My endless renditions,
Repeating poems with ambition,
Reading and editing, weeding out the bits that need to go,
Before I finish one, another has already come.
They breed, exceed my ability to write with speed,
I need to put the pen down and step away from the paper,
But still my mind is whirring it doesn't understand 'later'.
Poems starting to develop, occurring like tiny eggs.
I just write, they appear in spite of me.
They will hatch if I manage to catch the sonnet and the
   phonic words, the haiku and the stanzas and the
   subtleties of language.
I am inclined to just refuse, choose not to produce any more,
   throw down my pen, go on strike, make a picket
   line of consonants, be anarchic with alliteration
   and handcuff some couplets to a barbed wire
   fence.
But I don't think it would succeed, creativity
   would win over my negativity, trample on my
   placard and force me back to work.
Actually, it's ok because I would miss my nemesis,
I must embrace it and appreciate this ability before it is too
   late, before writer's block becomes my fate.
Then I'll be begging for the poems to return so excuse me,
   rude I do not mean to be but I must go and write
   some proper poetry.

Only Sunshine

I know there will be rain, heavy rain fall,
But I will crawl beneath you and be sheltered from it all.
When it's cold,
I'll fold myself under your coat,
Warm and dry, next to you I'll lie.
And when it snows, I'll hardly know,
I'll be cuddled up with you,
Cosy with just us two.
I will not notice blizzards or hail,
Whether the sun in his sky has turned pale,
I'll not notice if the puddles grow in size,
Or if the wind whirls around the skies,
If there is thunder and lightning.
To me it will be silent, it will not be frightening,
I will not realise that the moon has fallen to the ground,
Or that that the stars have been shot,
Without making a sound,
That the ocean has dried up,
Leaving just the seabed,
I'll only know what's in my sight and in my head,
And all I know is you,
And nothing else is real.
So, wind, snow, hail, storms just call my name,
And I'll feel the warmth of sunshine once again.

Harvest of Love

Bountiful, ripe, fruit laden love.
Harvest overflowing, fields glowing with haystacks and
        sunshine,
Reflection makes me sigh.
Where loneliness went, I do not care.
This love that is goodness, such pleasure that goes on
        forever,
For mile after mile, nothing higher or longer,
I certainly know of nothing stronger.
Tables laid out for a feast, platters of cheeses, bread and
        meats,
This feast for lovers, dishes piled with desserts and sweet
        treats,
Such luxurious love.
This love is good, respectful and fair.
My heart swells, like the gooseberries waiting patiently,
It is hard to comprehend that you chose me.
Exotic fruits all ripe and ready to eat,
Flesh just like the kisses you give, so sweet.
I am nothing special, have no riches to give,
Yet you say you will stay as long as you live,
And for some reason I believe you,
I see the truth in your eyes,
There is a sincerity about you, you cannot disguise.
You satisfy me completely, I will never be hungry again,
I am happy by your side as we sow new seeds of love.

They will grow so tall and healthy, and we will pick them
from the ground.
Each one will be perfectly formed, just like the love we have
found.
I came here with nothing, now I have so much,
I have your smile, I have your touch,
I have righteous love, fields of flower,
Towers of corn waving in the breeze,
Time together with comfort and ease.
Never will this soil reject, this love ever stop,
I have a love harvest - a bumper crop.

Painting

Hands feel the canvas
Images forming
Fingers itching
Paint pouring
Colour on white
What a beautiful sight
Too dark in the sky
How to improve
Move onto spray
Play with the pressure
Dribble and lay another colour on top
What a mess you've made
Light starting to fade
Stop and look
Image is coming
Starting to make sense in my head
Black for eyes, lead black irises
Spray it more gold
Texture and mould
White for light
Hold tight
Stand back
And then pack up your paints
Wait till it dries
Then decide
If this one is good enough to survive.

I Love You

Sometimes I feel unlovable, but I can't deny what you give to
      me,
Not feasible to fake, mistake, disguise, tell lies for these
      many years.
It must be truth on your lips when you say I love you.
A wonderful blurring of romance and friendship,
My best mate, my lover, together by fate.
We have something that is the cream, the top, gold,
Nothing else made in this mould except me and you.
I will not hesitate to say I love you too,
And I'll tell you something else,
You bring me such happiness,
I am blessed.
I never imagined a future, peace, completion and that the
      hate in my head would cease to exist, but with
      you it cannot persist.
You silenced it.
I was damaged and hurt, but you took on me and my mess,
Kissed my wounds, gave me nurture and care, your healing
      caress.
I am good now, content, past resentment gone,
I am strong.
It's been so long, nothing and no one will break me again.
Thank you for your belief, for seeing my soul,
My heart was your goal and now it's your prize,
We are winners together, and despite sometimes still,

doubting myself,
I will not give up on this pure, organic, raw, this something
special,
We have found that is so honest and true,
You should know,
I really, completely and utterly, love you.

Born Again

What if death is not the end but the beginning?
What if we are in a stage of metamorphosis that comes
        before real life starts?
Like the caterpillar waiting to be the butterfly, or the
        foetus forming in the womb.
This life could be soil in which we are seeds, starting to grow,
And sprout but not ready to burst through the surface.
People think they are living, oblivious to the fact that they
        haven't yet been fully created.
People think they are dying, ready to face the afterlife when
        all they are doing is leaving the pre-life.
What if we are chickens not even hatched, flowers still in
        bud, fish roe, un-ripened fruit?
We are not even breathing for ourselves, too young for
        independence, too fragile to function alone.
Imagine if old-age is just the stage before we shed our skin
        like corn snakes ready to expose our shiny new
        bodies.
Perhaps our bones are what we leave behind like shells
        abandoned on the seashore?
Will we walk away from those outer casings or fly away or
        swim away or will we do something that we could
        never yet think of?
What if you and I are mere thoughts in the creative
        imagination, notes scribbled on a pad, half-
        hearted ideas in the mind of a genius?

Still to be made, yet to be developed, neurons waiting,
        ready to spark up like fireworks that will shoot off
        like pink sherbet.
What if life is not about the end, but is about the beginning?
What if we are not yet born?

Hope for my Telescope

I bought you a telescope in the hope that you would view the
moons and stars,
Galaxies, meteors, Pluto and Mars,
That you would look beyond all this and dream of us up
there in bliss.
We could embrace, whilst sitting on a shooting star.
What a way to travel, we'd go far
Away from all these folk
Whose stupidity does evoke such irritation.
I'd rather be on a rocket station, waiting to be fired into
space,
I will gaze into your face and kiss your lips real slow,
As the rocket engines glow, we'll look into each other's eyes,
As we lift off, 'I love you,' I will say.
As we reach the Milky Way, you will hold me tight,
And we will become part of the night,
Stardust sprinkled upon the moon's ambient light.

A Celebration of You

If I were to celebrate you, I would hold a party in the sky,
Invitations would be delivered by fireflies.
You would arrive on a golden goat with your name
emblazoned on its coat.
You would be serenaded by a thousand orca whales, their
tails plucking the strings of harps, carved into the
shape of hearts.
Your dress made by mermaids from blue lace, sleeves of silk
sit on your milky skin.
A field mouse would place a neon crown upon your head,
Your entrance lit by trillions of luminescent creatures from
the seabed.
Inside, flora and fauna would fill every corner of the room,
Standing zebras make stripes and ribboned kites fly free,
Raspberry canes line the walls, heavy and tall with berries to
eat, making the scene complete.
Sloths in trees that would slowly take your coat.
A moat of liquid chocolate surrounds a dance floor made
from a giant custard cream.
I dream of dancing with you.
Penguins would wait tables shuffling with buckets of ice,
slices of lemon, fine wine and free-flowing champagne,
Suspended rain clouds releasing sweets upon the crowds
below,
Light shows by glow-worms take turns with dancing swans,
performing ballet on miniature ponds.

The dinner, served in the moonlight,
The delight of sandwiches stuffed with fish fingers and
        mayonnaise,
Eaten whilst a giraffe in a silver scarf plays the piano,
A font of yoghurt, fruit and honey dished out by baby
        bunnies,
Chocolate macaroons handed round by tuxedoed raccoons,
A dolphin DJ plays 80's tunes, whilst flamingo float around
        the room on pink balloons,
Cheering cheetahs and clapping seals give after dinner
        speeches that recognise your talent and wonder.
It would carry on longer than a week, and before we go it
        would end with a slow dance.
I see the smile on your face as we embrace.
The only thing worth partying for, which I should appreciate
        more, is you,
My love, whom I cannot wait to celebrate.

Chapter 7

When You See the Funny Side of Life

I don't like it when people take my Parkinson's too seriously. Yes, it's rubbish but, frankly, I'd rather be teased for it than have people feeling sorry for me. And trust me, there are a lot of jokes you can make out of this disease.

It's also not the worst thing that can happen, look around and be grateful for what you have, rather than focussing on what you don't.

I think a sense of humour helps us get through life and we all need something to assist us with that.

Life is funny, people are funny, laughing and having fun is good for you.

So, I thought I'd put in something a little humorous to end this with.

The Perspective of a Cow that Spends its Life Upon a Slope

The perspective of a cow that spends its life upon a slope,
Will be very different to one that lives in a shed or tied to a
rope in a flat field.
It will have a lovely view you see,
But on a slope, it's tricky to look, to be stable on all four
hooves.
It must be cautious when it moves,
It cannot run free without concern,
Or a heavy lesson it would learn.
It has to perfect a sideways walk,
Shuffle like a crab,
Watch its step, just like a hawk.
This caution makes a cow that lives on a slope want to leave,
run free, elope!
It dreams of living on the flat, of eating grass and getting fat,
Without a care it would be a cow so radiant,
But for now, it has to accept, the reality of the gradient.

Teams Call

I accepted the Teams call at ten to ten
Which is when
I had heard that familiar ring
More familiar than my phone or text ping
An alarm went off in my brain
Work, must get it straight away
Teams calls should be answered 24hours a day
I could see it was the boss
And to be honest I do give a toss
Because though I'd like to be glib
It would be a big fib
Coz she pays my wages
And life comes in stages
I'm trying to get to the one where life is more fun
The one where the mortgage is paid, the loan is done
But I'm not at that stage yet
So, I hastily get
From one room to another
To respond to big brother
And I press the camera pic too
Forgetting I'd just been to the loo
Completely naked
Not a stich had I on
When I'd gone
And answered the Teams call
To the Director

I felt such a fool
She laughed and said
'My you're looking fine
Why don't you ring me back
At a more convenient time.'

One Time Passcode Rage

One Time Passcode,
Resend to my device,
Now you've sent it twice.
Which OTP should I use?
Of course - whichever one I don't choose.
It flashed up, now it's gone from my screen,
Hidden itself just to be mean,
But what if I'm not with my phone?
Sorry can't compute – not with your phone?
This situation is unknown.
Now back to the start once more,
I have to enter my log in,
And I cannot remember my sodding pin.
What special bloody character?
Like Spider Man or Cinderella?
I put in the required capital letter,
It says the strength of your password could be better,
Send the OTP again.
Take a deep breath and count to ten.
The OTP does not work,
This computer is a jerk.
'You arsehole Dell thing you're not being fair,'
I'm shouting at my laptop, like it will care.
'Keep your dirty secrets, it's only Tesco's shopping,
I'll go to the 8 till late then let's see who'll win,
Coz I've got arms and legs and can go out of the house,

You're stuck inside with your OTPs and your pet bloody
        mouse.
I might forget my passwords and my username,
But I'm not a wanna be Apple, whose memory is lame.
When I got you, I thought you were fun,
That's it, one more OTP and we are done.
You know you should be careful, you could easily be sold,
I could buy something fancy,
Named after fruit in rose bloody gold.
Another OTP request comes in,
I shake my fist and as I approach the bin, laptop in hand,
I have the last word before it lands,
'Keep your virtual baskets and your f'ing sign in page,
I'm leaving,
I'm off in the car to experience some road rage!'

I Wish I had a Tank

I do not wish for chocolate,
I'll not ask for holidays or money in the bank.
No, if I had a wish,
I would wish for a proper military tank.
I would drive it down the High Street,
Past the bus stop where the kids meet,
I would drive it everywhere,
Past the windows of the shops selling ladies' wear,
I'd stop outside the chippy and buy a bag of chips,
I'd eat them with my head out of the top,
People wouldn't stop and stare,
Because with my rocket launchers pointed at them,
They wouldn't hang around, they wouldn't dare.
I'd probably get a discount in the Co-op if I asked,
And I bet the traffic wardens would just walk right on past,
Even if I parked outside the pub on a double yellow line,
So, I could stop for some peanuts and a glass of cold white
                    wine.
I'd overtake cyclists and, if they were not single file,
I'd point my rockets at them too, just for a little while.
I'd go to the care home where the old people reside,
I'd take them out in my big green tank for a Sunday drive.
I'd let them take control and go wherever they want to go,
Over fields, bumping along, I would not tell them to go slow.
If I had a tank, life would be such fun,
With caterpillar tracks and my big gun,

The people of Steyning would think I was crazy, kookie,
But I don't have a nice big tank, only a little red Suzuki.

Acknowledgements

This book is dedicated to J, without whom there would be no love. Dr Seuss for the inspiration. Toni, my biggest fan and poetry buddy who helped me enormously. My NBF whose honesty was refreshing and whose teaching was invaluable...and my mum, for passing on her creativity.

Love you all

The Real Press
Poetry without boundaries

You can see our full range of books here at
www.therealpress.co.uk

Printed in Great Britain
by Amazon